Evolution&
Revolution

Chinese Dress
1700s ~ 1990s

edited by Claire Roberts

Powerhouse Publishing

part of the Museum of Applied Arts and Sciences

First published 1997
Powerhouse Publishing, Sydney

Powerhouse Publishing
part of the Museum of Applied Arts and Sciences
PO Box K346 Haymarket NSW 1238 Australia
The Museum of Applied Arts and Sciences incorporates the
Powerhouse Musuem and Sydney Observatory.

Project management: Julie Donaldson, Powerhouse
Designer: Deborah Brash/Brash Design Pty Ltd
Text editor: Mary Rennie
Powerhouse photography: Penelope Clay, Scott Donkin,
Marinco Kojdanovski, Sue Stafford
Index: Caroline Colton

Printing and Colour Separations by
National Capital Printing, Canberra
Produced in QuarkXpress in Caslon and Frutiger

National Library of Australia
Cataloguing-in-Publication

Evolution & revolution: Chinese dress 1700s-1990s
Bibliography.
Includes index.
ISBN 1 86317 067 7

1. Costume – China – History. 2. Costume – Taiwan –
History. 3. Costume – Hong Kong – History. 4. Chinese –
Costume. 5. Hong Kong – Costume. 6. Taiwan – Costume.
7. Costume – Social aspects. I. Roberts, Claire, 1959-.

391.00951

Published in conjunction with the exhibition *Evolution &
revolution: Chinese dress 1700s to now* at the Powerhouse
Museum 25 June 1997 – May 1998 sponsored by SBS and
The Sunday Telegraph and supported by the Australia-China
Council.

(Image overleaf) Cover of a pattern book published during the
Cultural Revolution by the Research Studio of the Qingdao
Clothing Industry Company in 1968. It features Mao Zedong and
an inscription of his calligraphy which reads 'Serve the People'.
Courtesy of Sang Ye.

Acknowledgments

Many people have contributed to the preparation of the exhibition and this publication. I would like to particularly thank the Powerhouse Museum director, Terence Measham, for his support of this project; and Sang Ye, who was commissioned to source and research a collection of post 1949 mainland Chinese dress on behalf of the museum, and who has worked closely with me.

I would like to thank museum staff who have worked on this project and to lenders, designers, contributing authors and translators. Special thanks are extended to Carl Andrew, Dr Geremie R Barmé (senior fellow, Institute of Advanced Studies, Australian National University); Dr and Mrs E Cheong; Mandy Crook (assistant curator, Asian decorative arts and design, Powerhouse Museum); Zelda Cawthorne; Peter Coyne; Susan Dewar; Bruce Doar; Dr Feng Chongyi (lecturer in China studies, University of Technology, Sydney); Terrence N Fern; Graham Fletcher (cultural counsellor, Australian Embassy, Peking); Valery Garrett; Chris Hall; Dr James Hayes; Alice Hsu and Lin Li-chin (Taiwan Taipei Fashion Designers' Association, Taipei); Fay Hwang (formerly of the Australian Commerce and Industry Office, Taipei); Herta Imhof; Sally Ingleton (Singing Nomad Productions, Melbourne); Nicholas Jose; Dr Daniel Kane (cultural counsellor, Australian Embassy, Peking); Ping-hong Lau; Li Xin (China Garment Designers' Association, Peking); Hannah Pang; Dr Mae-Anna Pang (senior curator of Asian art, National Gallery of Victoria); Judith and Ken Rutherford; Dr Gene Sherman; Ann Stephen; Christina Sumner; Bronwyn Thomas; Neil Thompson; Hiram To; Sue Trevaskes; Zoe Wang; Wang Youshen; Linda Wrigglesworth; Xu Hong; Mimi Yeung, Patrick Lam and Agnes Chan (Hong Kong Trade Development Council, Hong Kong); Kevin Yeung (Hong Kong Fashion Designers' Association); and Zhou Xiaowei.

Claire Roberts

Note on Chinese language

The *pinyin* system of romanising Mandarin Chinese has been followed with the exception of commonly accepted local place names such as Peking instead of Beijing and Canton instead of Guangzhou; and Cantonese terms, such as *cheungsam*, which is used in preference to the Mandarin *qipao* in the essays on dress in Hong Kong. For the essay on Taiwanese dress, the Wade-Giles system of transliteration has been followed. To assist the reader with pronouncing Chinese names and terms the following guide is provided:

c = ts (*caifeng = ts'ai feng*); q = ch (*Qing = Ch'ing*); x = sh (*xuesheng fu = hsüeh sheng fu*).

为人民服务

服装量裁

青岛市服装工业公司研究室编印

Contents

Foreword

Evolution & revolution: Chinese dress 1700s–1990s has been published to coincide with the inaugural exhibition in the Powerhouse Museum's new Asian gallery. The exhibition and the book, both initiated by the Powerhouse Museum, represent a unique contribution to our understanding of Chinese society by examining change in Chinese culture through the medium of dress with an emphasis on the last 100 years.

The Powerhouse Museum holds one of Australia's foremost collections of dress and an important Asian collection of decorative arts and design, the development of which can be traced back to the Sydney International Exhibition of 1879. Since the establishment of the museum in 1880, the Asian collection has grown steadily and now numbers some 10 000 objects.

Our choice of subject for the inaugural exhibition related to four factors: the strength of the museum's Chinese collection, the museum's location adjacent to Sydney's Chinatown, the history of Australia's relationship with China, and the historic transition of Hong Kong sovereignty from Britain to the People's Republic of China on 1 July 1997.

One of the principal aims of the gallery, together with publications and educational programs, is to make aspects of Asian cultures more accessible to Australian audiences. Dress is something that is common to us all and encoded within it is information about the society in which we live. By choosing to explore Chinese culture through changes in dress design we have sought a friendly medium through which aspects of Chinese history and culture can be more readily understood.

I am grateful to the many people in Australia, mainland China, Hong Kong, Taiwan and Britain who have generously assisted the museum with the development and realisation of this project. Particular thanks are extended to lenders and to the exhibition sponsors — SBS and *The Sunday Telegraph* — and for the assistance from the Australia–China Council.

I wish to acknowledge the many staff who have contributed to this publication and the exhibition. In particular I wish to thank Claire Roberts, curator of Asian decorative arts and design for her hard work in establishing the Asian gallery and assistant curator Mandy Crook who has worked closely with her on all aspects of the project over the past year.

Finally, I would like to pay tribute to our Board of Trustees for the substantial support they have provided for this important new initiative. In this regard, I mention Dr John Yu, who was a Trustee for many years until very recently; Dr Gene Sherman; and the president Mr Jim Spigelman QC.

Terence Measham
Director, Powerhouse Museum

(Opposite page) Advertising poster for B & M Company Fertiliser, colour lithograph by Zhou Baisheng, made in Shanghai, China during the late 1930s.
Powerhouse Museum collection.

Introduction

The concept of dress is common to us all. By wrapping our bodies in layers of cloth, we protect the skin and preserve our modesty. In dress we construct an identity which reflects status and aspects of the time in which we live, highlighting or concealing tradition, ideology, the state, an employer, fashion houses or the marketplace — although individual style has always been an important modifier. Dress is intimately connected to social life and to the cultural history of place — to the beliefs, aspirations and the self-expression of the individual and society.

Within Chinese society, dress has long been a way to identify people's position within the social hierarchy. The Chinese character *fu* means clothing or dress. But that same Chinese character has a wide range of other connotations, including to serve, to obey, and even to be in mourning. There exists the closest relationship between clothing and ritual, in today's language, social standing, functions and duties. As these connotations and meanings suggest, the individual and the body are subjugated to particular social needs.

This book explores changes in Chinese culture through the medium of dress and in particular the impact that social, cultural, political and economic forces have exerted on dress design. The focus is on urban dress in the major centres of population, government, industry and trade. Peking, Shanghai, Canton, Hong Kong and Taipei are major cities which have led the changes in dress for much of the period under discussion — from the beginning of the Qing (Ch'ing) dynasty to the present.

Essays have been commissioned from writers in Australia, mainland China, Hong Kong and Taiwan in order to present histories of Chinese dress from both Chinese and Western perspectives. A number of writers have drawn on extensive oral-history research highlighting, in very poignant ways, the relationship between history and material culture. The emphasis on twentieth-century Chinese dress and contemporary fashion makes this project both striking and unique.

Claire Roberts

(Opposite page) Young boy paying respects to his parents and ancestors at the family shrine during Chinese New Year. The father wears a long robe (*changpao*), riding jacket (*magua*) and skullcap; the mother wears a jacket and trousers (*aoku*); and the son a long robe.

Gelatin silver photograph by Hedda Morrison, Peking 1933-46. Powerhouse Museum collection. Gift of Alastair Morrison, 1992.

(*duanzhao*) over his semi-formal robe. Only the emperor's sons, imperial princes and highest ranking officials were authorised to also wear this coat — and then only with the emperor's permission.

The emperor's semi-formal surcoat (*gunfu*) could only be worn on the occasion of ceremonial sacrifices to heaven or when making votive offerings to secure a rich harvest or bountiful rain. It was azure coloured with a rounded neckline, opened at the centre front, and reached to the hips, although in the late Qing period it could extend to below the knee. The surcoat was decorated with four gold-dragon medallions and featured five engraved gold buttons. The emperor's surcoat had symbols of the sun and moon on each shoulder. Identical surcoats, minus the insignia of the sun and moon, were worn by the emperor's sons and termed *longgua* rather than *gunfu*. When the emperor or any of his sons wore these surcoats, civil and military court officials wore similar surcoats (*bufu*), which differed in that the court insignia on the front and back indicated the rank of the wearer. The surcoats of male members of the royal family displayed round central badges (*buzi*), whereas those of the civil and military officials were square.

★ Emperor's azure surcoat (*gunfu*), with four dragon medallions embroidered in gold-wrapped thread on satin-weave silk made in China about 1800. The shoulder medallions feature representations of the sun and moon.

Chris Hall Collection Trust, Jobrenco Ltd Trustee. Photo by Sue Stafford.

The court insignia badges on surcoats of the princes of perpetual inheritance designated 'princes of the blood' (*qinwang*) featured four dragon medallions, a profile dragon on each shoulder and a front-facing dragon on the front and back. The surcoats of princes of perpetual inheritance designated *junwang*, a rank of nobility next to prince, featured four five-clawed profile dragon medallions; and Manchu princes (*beile*), a rank of the Manchu nobility below that of the prince, wore two four-clawed dragon medallions.

The surcoats of civil and military officials displayed square court insignia badges with emblems designating one of the nine possible ranks: a crane for first rank; a golden pheasant for second; a peacock for third; a wild goose for fourth; a silver pheasant fifth; an egret sixth; a *xichi* — an ancient bird resembling a mandarin duck — seventh; a quail eighth; and a paradise flycatcher the ninth rank. The court insignia badges on a censor's surcoat featured the *xiezhi* — a mythical beast resembling a dragon-headed mastiff. Court insignia badges for military officials of

★ **Men's black surcoat (*bufu*), for a second-rank civil official, with embroidered golden pheasant court insignia badges attached front and back on damask-weave satin, made in China during the late 1800s.**

Private collection. Photo by Penelope Clay.

the first rank featured a *qilin*, sometimes regarded as a Chinese unicorn; of the second, a lion; the third, a leopard; the fourth, a tiger; the fifth, a bear; the sixth, a panther; the seventh and eighth, a rhinoceros; and the ninth, a sea horse (*haima*). The rank insignia on the jackets of agricultural officials featured stylised roseate clouds surrounding the sun.

The rank insignia on the clothing of wives of officials conformed to those of their husbands, although wives of military officials displayed the equivalent bird rather than an animal, suggesting the gentility of women.

★ Court insignia badge for a fifth-rank military official, silk and gold-wrapped thread tapestry weave (*kesi*). This badge depicts a bear and would have been attached to the rear of a miltary official's surcoat (*bufu*); made in China during the mid 1800s.

Powerhouse Museum collection. Gift of Miss E A McDonald, 1971. Photo by Sue Stafford.

Semi-formal or festive wear for court officials included hats which were frequently decorated with peacock-feather attachments indicating rank. There were three main types of feather: the *hualing*, *lanling* and *ranlaning*. The *hualing* indicated noble rank, and could have one, two or three 'eyes' — the greater number of 'eyes' indicating a more elevated rank.

Semi-formal or festive wear for court women, such as the emperor's wife and mother, and the various ranks of concubine, comprised a dragon surcoat (*longgua*), a dragon robe (*longpao*) worn beneath the surcoat, and a semi-formal court hat. The dragon surcoat featured a round neck with a centre-front opening and side slits. It was the same length as the semi-formal court robe. There were three styles of female dragon robe (*longpao*): those decorated with nine gold dragons and with the eight-treasure deep-water pattern (*babao lishui*) forming the lower section of the robe; the same design but with eight gold-dragon medallions; and those with eight gold-dragon medallions and the lower half undecorated.

The informal surcoat for men in the Qing court consisted of a knee-length centre-front opening coat with a round neck, but no court insignia badge. There were no restrictions on the embroidered decoration.

Travelling dress and wet-weather dress

Travelling dress comprised a riding jacket (*magua*) fastened at the centre front with five buttons, under which a riding gown (*xingshang*) was worn. The riding gown crossed over at the front to fasten on the right; had four splits to the skirt — at the sides, front and back; and was also shorter on the right for convenience when riding. This outfit was teamed with a riding hat and riding belt — from which hung a range of purses; perfume sachets; a long rectangular bag with an opening in the middle for money and other small items (*dalian*); a bag containing a lighter (*huolian*); fan case; and optional extras such as a flint (*sui*), bodkin for untying knots (*xi*), knife, scraper, compass, a container for toothpicks, and a kerchief made from Koryo (Korean) cloth.

Wet-weather wear consisted of a rain hat, rain clothes and raincoat fashioned from heavily oiled silk (*youchou*), black sateen (*yuduan*) or camlet (*yusha*).

Manchu women's dress

The wives of Qing officials bearing titles conferred by the emperor wore a sleeveless vest called a *xiapei* over a three-quarter length jacket and a skirt. In the centre of the vest was a court insignia badge depicting the emblem that conformed to their husband's rank.

★ Cantonese mandarin and his wife, photographed by M Miller, about 1861-64. The civil official wears a formal court robe (*chaofu*) and surcoat (*bufu*) displaying his rank, together with *piling* collar and ceremonial court beads (*chaozhu*). His wife wears a sleeveless vest (*xiapei*) over a jacket and skirt. Her feet are bound indicating that she is Han Chinese.

Courtesy of the Royal Asiatic Society, London.

When Manchu women wore semi-formal dress rather than formal dress, they wore hair ornaments instead of hats. For informal wear, they wore their hair in what was called the 'Manchu Banner bun' (*qiji*) style, which required the hair to be parted in the middle and fixed into two flat, round buns on each side of the head at brow level. A long and wide jade hairpin called a *bianfang* was then passed through the buns at the back of the head to hold the hair in place. The shape of the horizontal jade hairpin resembled the Chinese word or character 'one', and so the hairstyle was sometimes called 'the character one hairstyle' (*yizitou*). By the reign of the Daoguang Emperor (1821–1850), a small frame was used to support and raise the coiffure, and the hairstyle came to be known as *jiazitou*. In the

★ Women's vest (*xiapei*), silk and gold-wrapped thread embroidery on silk, made in China in the late 1800s. The court insignia badge displays a silver pheasant, indicating that the vest would have been worn by the wife of a fifth-rank civil official.

Powerhouse Museum collection. Photo by Sue Stafford.

3 5

Before joining up I was an urchin; the child of a poor peasant family. I'd seen but never worn 'foreign cloth' (*yangbu*), the type of machine-woven material that everyone goes around in these days. Generally, I only got to wear the clothes that my elder brother had outgrown. Even when I did get a new piece of clothing at New Year, it was of the homespun cloth made at home.

Even though I was going off to join the Revolution, walking along a golden path to the future, I was still abandoning home, and my mother was unhappy to let me go. She didn't prevent me from leaving; after all, she was a liberated peasant herself, so she was politically aware. But so as to give me a parting gift she got all the money she had saved from selling chicken eggs — the peasant's bank is the bum of a chicken — took my measurements and had a friend in the county seat get this robe tailored for me.

I remember it really clearly: when she went to pick it up she discovered she didn't have enough money, so an old hen had to be thrown in to complete the deal. When she brought it back she couldn't stop looking at it and feeling it; she was so delighted! She made me try it on any number of times, muttering all the while: 'No wonder it hangs so beautifully, it is, after all, "foreign cloth". You look so well-dressed in it, just like an educated gentleman.'

The whole village came out to see me off, accompanying the procession with cymbals and drums. When we reached the edge of the village my mother started crying. She said through a veil of tears: 'Go on then, don't think of us. Follow Chairman Mao and fight your way to Nanjing. Capture Chiang Kai-shek alive!'

Today my children don't understand how people felt back then, what the Revolution was all about. But that's how people were. The head of my village tied a big red cloth flower to my chest as I left.

In the end, I didn't get much use out of the robe. I wore it from my village to the county seat and then to Shijiazhuang. Once I joined up with the army I had to put on a mustard-coloured army uniform. But I kept my robe with me in my rucksack, taking it with me when I crossed the Yellow River, and again over the Yangtse, as well as when we crossed the straits to Hainan Island in the south. Many of my comrades gave the clothing they had worn when they joined up to people they met along the way or just threw it away. But I couldn't bring myself to do that. Whenever I look at it I think of my old mother — the way she felt it all over, how much she liked it, how happy she was with the way I looked when I put it on …

Although it is a memento, I'm happy for you to use it in your exhibition. My daughter said that you were looking for a piece of clothing that symbolised the gulf between two different periods. Well you've found what you've been looking for. Take it.

Translated by Geremie R Barmé.

Making foreign things serve China

*An 83-year-old tailor reflecting on the fate of the Western suit in revolutionary China. He is a member of the last generation of new-style tailors from Fenghua in Zhejiang Province (*Fengbang caifeng*). These tailors are renowned for their modifications of the Zhongshan zhuang (*Sun Yat-sen suit*).*

When you work with clothes, you can do just about anything with them. Western suits, for example, can be transformed into revolutionary uniforms. The tailors where I worked, the Western District Clothing Cooperative, did just that.

Western-style suits were remnants from the Old Society, and the people who wanted them transformed generally had money to pay for the tailoring; although state cadres who were sent overseas also came to us — they too had to wear suits on official occasions.

From the early 1950s, we had a lot of requests to remodel suits. Back then materials were expensive but labour was cheap, and it only cost a few *yuan* to re-fashion a suit. So lots of tailors provided this particular service. They'd advertise it with a sign on the counter or hanging outside which read: 'Reconditioning of Western Suits' (*Fanxiu xifu*).

Uniforms (*zhifu*) were recognised as the mark of state employees; to wear one was to be progressive. If you wore a suit people thought you were a capitalist, an interpreter or somebody who'd returned from overseas. The student uniform (*xuesheng fu*) was not dignified enough, not formal. Young people could get away with wearing them, but they were unsuitable for older people.

★ **(Above) Man's uniform jacket (*zhifu*) re-fashioned in the 1950s from a navy-blue Western-style woollen suit.**

Powerhouse Museum collection. Photo by Sue Stafford.

★ **(Right) Detail of 1950s man's uniform jacket (*zhifu*) showing the ingenious way a Chinese tailor re-fashioned the Western-style suit by re-cutting and piecing together small pieces of fabric, only obvious in the areas that were not exposed when the garment was worn.**

Powerhouse Museum collection. Photo by Sue Stafford.

You had to follow the fashion and, in clothing, the model was Chairman Mao. He wore a uniform [either the *zhifu*, or a modified Sun Yat-sen suit]. What good was it to emulate Lu Xun [the 1920s–1930s left-wing writer]. He was of the old school, he wore a student uniform or a long robe.

For the first few years after Liberation no one changed, and although people didn't wear suits to work, you would see them on Sundays or when people visited each other. If you had the money, you just put them to be seen getting married in such an ensemble. Those who would were people who liked getting dressed up, who cared what they looked like, minor actresses like me, or nurses. We were thought of as being politically suspect, for clinging to the Four Olds [ideas, culture, customs and habits]. The head of my troupe criticised me: 'Generally you behave like a revolutionary fighter on the arts front, but on your wedding day you really did look like a rotten bourgeois trollop. It wasn't good.'

And that, for the time, was pretty courteous. At least he didn't accuse me of having dressed up like a landlord's concubine. Having the daring to wear something like that

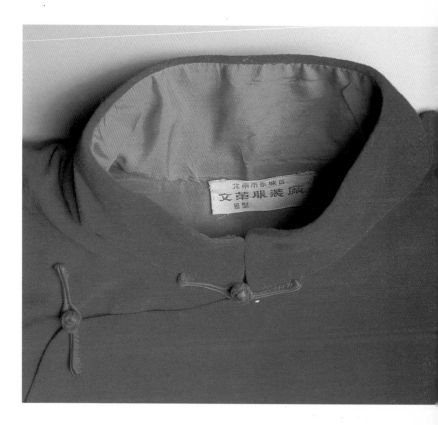

★ Detail of woman's wedding jacket (*xiao'ao*), purchased by the owner in 1977, showing the manufacturer's label — Cultural Revolution Garment Factory, Peking.

Powerhouse Museum collection. Photo by Scott Donkin.

was only half of it. There was also the question of whether you thought it was worth the expense. At the time, after all, people had very low incomes, not like today when you can go shopping and buy something on the spot. Back then you really had to think carefully about whether an item of clothing was practical; whether you could wear it both at work and in your time off. So many people felt that since you wouldn't be wearing it again after you got married, it wasn't worth the cost. The price of 'buying face' was far too high.

And I didn't wear it much after I got married. Don't forget the year was 1977. If I went out in this top I would have really stood out in the crowd. People would have thought I was soft in the head.

Nor could I wear it to other people's weddings. Wedding guests always wore uniforms (*zhifu*); if I wore this then everyone would have spent their time staring at me instead of the bride. Anyway, most brides wore uniforms, too. It would have made things very uncomfortable for them if I'd worn it.

Nor did I get much of a chance to use it after the government's Open Door Policy was introduced [in 1979]. In the 1980s and '90s, fashions in clothes and colours have changed rapidly; the centre of attention is Paris, New York and Hong Kong. Only hotel floor managers would ever wear anything like this nowadays. Now it's their uniform. Anyway, I'm a bit past it now. Old mums like me aren't in any position to be fashion trendsetters. So I just got to indulge myself in this jacket once.

Translated by Geremie R Barmé.

1lb

CHINESE
DRIED LICHEE